WORKING ON LIVING

IMAGINATION AND WONDER

DONALD SWOFFORD

LifeRich
PUBLISHING

Scripture taken from the King James Version of the Bible

LifeRich Publishing is a registered trademark of The Reader's Digest Association, Inc.

LifeRich Publishing books may be ordered through booksellers or by contacting:

LifeRich Publishing
1663 Liberty Drive
Bloomington, IN 47403
www.liferichpublishing.com
1 (888) 238-8637

ISBN: 978-1-4897-1124-3 (sc)
ISBN: 978-1-4897-1123-6 (e)

Library of Congress Control Number: 2017904216

Print information available on the last page.

LifeRich Publishing rev. date: 05/23/2017

DEDICATION TO

Dolores A Alexander
Tracy D Swofford

INTRODUCTION

This book is based on faith. In hopes people will follow Jesus Christ's teachings. For many years, I have been wrighting down the poems and litature, that is in this book, not knowing why. Perhaps, I was going to be a preacher one day? Or a sunday school teacher? I had know idea. So, I kept doing what God was showing me, and wrighting down his message. I had notes, and papers, scattered everywhere. So, I got all of it together, and prayed, and I put what I got so far, in this book. Some of the book, I dreamed, and some were inspired. I'm not a preacher. I'm just doing what Christians are suppose to do. Spreading his word of truth. I hope you get something out of this book. Keep working on the living Christ. He will be here soon.

THE LIFE WE CHOOSE

For we are his workmanship, created in Christ Jesus for his good works, which God prepared beforehand that we should walk in them.

Ephesians 2:10

CHAPTER 1

Living In Space

Sometimes, I often wonder.
What I'm doing, way up here.
Away from my friends, and family.
The ones, I love, so dear.

The friends up here, their good to me.
As good, As good, can be.
But, I sure miss, the ones back home.
That mean so much to me.

My mother she is, very sick,
you know, not well at all.
By the phone, she'll surely wait.
Just waiting, for my call.

I'd like to see her very much.
To see her, smiling face.
If she could walk, like you and me.
That floor, I know, she'd pace.

Now, I've been here, and I've been there.
This country-side, I've roamed.
But, if I didn't know any better,
I'd rather be, back home.

[Foot Note,] Working on getting home.

(Mother to son, Son to mother)

I'm truly blessed, to have a son, like you.
I'm glad, I have a mom, to help me, when I'm blue.
I'll wipe away the tears, cause your, my little man.
I'm here for you, I will do, the best I can.

I will be there, to watch you, stand tall.
And, I will be there, to catch you, when you fall.
Remember, how I helped you, when you were in school.
I remember, you were there, when I acted, like a fool.

And, when you are sick, I'll always, be at your side.
I don't know what I'd ever do, if you'd ever die.
Now, don't be silly son, I'm not going anywhere.
I'll always have peace, in my heart, mom.
Because, I know you care.

I love you more, with each passing day.
I love you too mom, don't ever go away.

TESTIMONY

CHAPTER 2

We Are Own Our Own

(The Truth)

As the stories told, And, this story is told all over the world, And beyond. There are many books, and versions, on what people believe in. The way they worship, and how they pray, and, how they conduct their life, as they walk through their everyday living. Some say, All you got to do to get in heaven is, to be good. And some say you have to be perfect in Gods eyes. And some say, just love nature, and animals. And then, there are others, who say, All we got to do, is wait.

I myself, always try to keep an open mind, and a open heart, As a christian, I am not perfect, and I never claim to be. Neverthaless, I stand firm, on my believes. My faith is strong with the Lord. I have had many biblical dreams, and I've seen, and, heard, lots of small miracles from God. He guide's me, through my life.

I try to do Gods will. But, as you know, sometimes, thats hard. Knowing whats Gods will is, And dealing with our own arrigance. So, have faith in the Lord Jesus Christ, and be patient. He will guide you. In his own time. Don't treat faith, like fast food. Leave it in his hands. Jesus will guide you, and teach you, in his own time. And he always has, perfect timing.

FAITH, is what this book is based on. Its easy to say,
"I got faith," But, you really don't have faith, unless you really
love Jesus, deep inside. And you trust him. Wait, have patients
for your answer. In this fast moving world. People don't want
to wait, patients run thin. But, what some people don't
understand is, God, is in controll, of everything. He always
has, and always will, through the beginning of time, untill the
end of time. Have faith, in whatever you ask of him. There is
nothing he can't handle.

As we go through this life. Seeing our family members.
Visiting with our friends. Talking to our neighbors, or
having conversations with co-workers. These people, like
it or not, are in your life group. They know you. And what
kind of person you are. Good, or bad. Outsiders, on the
other hand, don't know you. And most are quick to judge.
There will always be at least one person, at a resturant, or
store, or the car wash, or the mall, or a game, anywhere in
public. they will be looking at you, and judge you on what
type of person you are. Your expression on your face, the
way you dress, or what you bought, or how you talk. most
people, ignore it. And it bothers some. The point is, Jesus,
is watching us 24/7. And he is taking notes.

Although, he knows how many hairs on your head, and
every bug you stepped on in your entire life, and everything
about you, since the day you were born. He knows you got
free will to do anything you want to do in your life. He
knows everything you said, and everything you did.

The good news is,

Know matter what you said or did, He still loves you.
HE LOVES YOU. There is nothing else in this world, or
in this universe he wants, is for you to love him. Thats it.
With the free will he gave you. That will make the Lord
Jesus Christ smile. He does not want to force you to love
him. He wants your love, openly. All on your on. With
all of your heart, mind, and soul. But, Jesus will love you.
Know matter what you do.

Praise him. Repent to him. In that order. He will guide
you, and teach you. All through your life. So, you can
be a better person. So, when ever your being watched,
by family, or friends, or co-workers, or in the public
eye. Your light will shine bright, for all to see...
Amen

TESTIMONY

CHAPTER 3

Lessons Learned

(A Future Life)

We tried to run. We tried to hide.
Thats how they found us, and pulled
us out from deep inside. We seen all
their stares. We seen all their looks.
Thats why we have God. Who wrote
them down, in his book.

[Foot Note] Right now, many people around the world, are being prosecuted
for being Christians. This little girl was hiding, and working on her faith.

(My Friend, "Bird")

I saw a bird, up in the sky.
He had one wing, I know not why.
I felt so sad, I began to cry.
He began to sing, And flew close by.

He sat right down, real close to me.
Began to speak, hard to believe.
He ask me, why I felt so blue?
I told him, cause I cry for you.
You have one wing, and sing and play.
And never, never cry this way.

He said, I'll tell you why, I have one wing.
And cause I play, and fly, and sing.
You see, forever, I have been this way.
The Lord, just gave me one that day.

He told me not to worry though.
That I would never fly to low.
He said, I am a special bird.
I talk to Jesus, and I heard his word.

Now, he's took real good care of me.
I'm healthy as a bird, you see.
We are all his children, birds are too.
And then I don't feel so blue.

He said, now don't you cry for me no more.
And, I'll be singing at your door.
He got up then, and flew away.
And I still see him, everyday.

So, just give thanks, to him up high.
and maybe, one day, we will fly...

[Foot Note] Working on being happy, no matter your handicap.

(The Wall)

We are all in prison, one way, or the other.
But, we can use our minds, and be undercover.
The wind will always blow, and time will always be set.
You can't controll the sunrise.
And, you can't controll the sunset.

But, if we can free our minds, of everyday stress.
Then maybe, in the future, we won't be in this mess.

(To My Love)

No matter where I go, when we are apart.
You are with me, and close to my heart.
It makes me feel good, to have feelings this way.
Thoughts of you, brightens my day.

The pains that you go through.
You know that I care.
The thoughts of losing you.
Is more than I can bare.

I want to make you happy.
All through your days.
I want to give you what you deserve.
I'm kinda funny that way.

TESTIMONY

CHAPTER 4

Forever Young

(No Time)

And the city had no need of the sun, and of
the moon, to shine in it. For the glory of God
did lighten it. And the Lamb is the light thereof.
Rev 21:23

Your thoughts, and your believes, is all we have
in this life. And everyone has an opinion. If you can
imagine for a moment, a place where there is no time,
or date. I believe in heaven, there is such a place, A
place where you don't need a watch, or clock, or
calender, or any other device that tells time. Can you
imagine? In this life, we need our time. It's apart of our
daily activitys. We would be in chaos, without it.
Think about it. We would not know what to do.

Jesus, went to prepare a place for you, and me.
If God can create the heavens and the universe, and
life itself, in his great wisdom. Can you imagine, what
type of place he's preparing for us?

If heaven has no time, why would you need, days
of the week? or years? The bible says, we would have
eternal life. For ever and ever. Theres no time in that
statement. Theres no time table, on how long we would
be in heaven. A never ending world of happiness, and
content.

Don't miss understand me. This is only my belief,
my opinions. It's only a theory I have. A theory, on
how great heaven is going to be. Therefore, I believe,
there is no time in heaven.

And there shall be no night there, and they need no
candle, niether light of the sun. For the Lord God
giveth them light. And they shall reign for ever and
ever. Rev 22:5

In the city walls of heaven, why would we need
time? the symbolism of the sun, is light. the symbol-
ism son, is light. the symbolism of God, is light. god
said, there shall be no night. It isn't that hard to bel-
ieve, when you consider that the oceans, and the skys
are mostly the same color. And the sun really never
goes away. Theres no time in heaven. And also, there
is no time in hell. Forever hated, forever in pain, for
eternity. forever and ever...

On the subject of all that light, and time will not exist. gives us another understanding, what it would be like in heaven. Maybe, just maybe, our eyes will be open for eternity, and we will never sleep. We will never get tired. If that would be the case, I wonder throughout eternity, would we progress? Grow? For- ever be the same? Living in Gods love? That would be fine with me. And these expressions, and theorys are just thoughts. Like a child using their imagination, On what it would be like, here in this life.

I found the time to wright this. In heaven, I will not need to find the time. There will be no time. As long as we like. To be with Jesus. Forever loved. For- ever content. Forever at peace. For eternity. Forever, and ever. Amen

TESTIMONY

CHAPTER 5

World Of Peace

(Heaven)

Your whole life will be wonderful, in a world you'll never want. There will be nothing you'll dislike. The landscape will be glories to behold. The smells will always be of fresh grass and fresh flowers. With the air so crisp. There always be a light on your face, and you'll never be in the dark. Your eyes will see many wonderful colors, that you never seen before. Everything you want, will always be at your finger tips. Nothing will ever die, And you will never have to worry, about tomorrow. Your mind will always be free, you will never have to worry. There will be no aches, and pains, You will be in perfect health. You will never cry, You will never be hungry. And you will always be satisfied, and You will always feel good. You will never need to watch over your shoulder, you will trust everything, and everybody around you. You will never fear, and you'll never be alone. Smiles, will be everywhere. there will always be a hand to hold.

Amen

TESTIMONY

CHAPTER 6

World Of chaos

(Hell)

There will be no hand to hold. The landscape will not look pretty. Your tears will flow every day. You won't be able to stop crying. You'll always be in pain, and you will never stop hurting. The sorrows of others, you will constantly hear. The suffering will go on everyday. You will hate where you are, and you will hate how you feel. Your pain, and your hurting, will be so great, you will not care about others. You will never escape it. It will be a part of your daily, and nightly life, for years on end. And you will wish to die.

But, you won't. You will always be hungry, and you will never be full. There will never be no relief. Your hurting will never quit. You will only think of yourself and knowone else. You will never know what day, or tomorrow will bring. you will always think, what life could have been, and what it is now. You will never change the past, and you won't be able to change the future. Thats how bad you will feel. And you will never lose that feeling. Amen

TESTIMONY

CHAPTER 7

World We Live In

(present)

We have both worlds, peace and chaos. But, either one doesn't last forever. God gives us a choice, of which world we want to live in. In this life, we have complete controll of our lives. God give us free will to do what we want, that makes us feel, happy, and content, in the way we live. Knowing that we will die one day. Some of us care, and some don't. We have met both, right? The attitudes, and the feelings, we have spent a lifetime, to make up who we are today. Everyone feels they are doing there part. But, for what degree of arrogance and pride? Some of us have questions that never get answered. And, some of us knows the answers, before the question is ask. Any question can be answered thru our Lord Jesus Christ. He is the only one who can help us in this world we live in. He can teach us how we want to spend our life in eternity. He is real. He is alive. He loves us, know matter of our past. He wants us to believe in him, and trust him, with our lives in this world we live in. A world of chaos? or a world of peace? Its our choice.

Amen

TESTIMONY

CHAPTER 8

How To Pray

(In Your Words)

Our father, who art in heaven.
Hallowed be thy name.
Thy kingdom come. Thy will be done
In earth, as it is in heaven. give
us this day, our daily bread, and forgive
our debts, as we forgive our debters.
And lead us not into temptation, But,
deliver us from evil: for thine is the kingdom,
and the power, and the glory, for ever
and ever. Amen Matt 6:9-13

TESTIMONY

_____

_____

_____

_____

_____

_____

_____

_____

_____

_____

_____

_____

_____

_____

_____

_____

_____

CHAPTER 9

Work With People

(Not 4 People)

Being a modern christian is really hard.
Your at work, more than your at home.
The hand is played, and seeds are sown.
Its the way it is, living in your dome.

Life goes on, when your not at home.
You hear the news, on your final drive.
Your family wants, and your bills to pay.
It never ends, as you try to survive.

If you live like this, Your doing it wrong.
You'll have doctor bills, with all that stress.
Your family, and friends will suffer the most.
You'll wonder, How can I get out of this mess.

Here's a thought, if you go with this plan.
don't work for anybody, just try to help.
The rewards will be great, you'll be a better man
Work with people, and your problems will melt.

Work with Jesus, he's got the right idea.
He knows what's right, he'll calm the beast.
Working for people, your like everybody else.
All God wants, is for you to live in peace.

TESTIMONY

CHAPTER 10

Don't Miss The Boat

(Long Ago)

Long ago, before the rains. An old grey bearded man was walking slowly with his bow, in the deep forest. He was a great hunter, and far from home. As he walked, ever so slowly. He heard a faint sound of hammering, the sound was beyond the trees.. He took out his wine skin, and took a small drink. listening more intently. He knew know one has ever lived, where the big oaks grow. Walking slowly, and holding his head up, an looking both ways. He followed the sound. He had to see who else was here. After a while. He came to a clearing out of the forest, and couldn't believe his eyes. He saw an older bearded man, setting high up, on a swing, hammering on a gigantic boat. He looked around, and said to himself, Theres no water here for miles. He took out an apple, and set on a stump, ate the apple, and watched him curiously for a bit. Then, got up, and walked back into the forest, and headed home. He had to tell the others what he saw.

After a while. on his way back. He saw some strange tracks on the ground. He knew these woods very well, and never saw tracks like these. It spooked him a little. He stood up, and looked both ways, and saw nothing. He continued walking, looking both ways. Hour later, He saw, two mules, with black and white stripes all over them. This great hunter, has never saw an animal like this. He took careful aim with his bow, but, could not shoot them. The creature's seem to ignor him. As they walked out of sight, deeper in the forest. The hunter rushed back to town to tell what he saw. He told a group of men his story, and they laughed at him. He told everyone in town, and they laughed. They wanted to drink from his wine skin, because they knew it had to be something special. The hunter got really mad, and said in a loud voice. Follow me unbelievers, and I will show you. And they did.

A large crowd aproached the gigantic boat. They saw the old man hammering away, and ask him, HEY, WHAT ARE YOU DOING? The old grey bearded man stop hammering, and looked at the crowd of people, and said, COME JOIN ME, THE GREAT WATERS ARE COMING. They laughed and mocked him. They knew he had to be insane. Weeks went by, and people from all around came to watch. Everyday, they laughed, and mocked him and they dranked, and they watched strange creatures enter the boat. Before the old grey bearded man shut the huge door, he said again, JOIN ME. They laughed and mocked him again. As he shut the huge door. It started to rain.

When God told Noah to build a boat, because he was going to flood the earth. Noah knew he had a hard job ahead of him, and at first, he didn't believe it either. Most people in this generation can't even amagine how really hard that job was. Not to mention, people mocking you while you work. Trying to get it done, before the deadline. The outsiders watching could not believe him, even though they seen the hard work, And all the strange animals they seen. An old story, that most people today, still don't believe. To me, that says alot about people who don't believe in God today. One day, the whole world will know about all the hard working people, you and me, and all the people, that are in the bible.

If you see someone working hard on something, and it looks stupid to you, and every one else. Help them to achive there goals. You might be rewarded in the end. And, who knows, You might be working for God.

TESTIMONY

CHAPTER 11

Friendship

You don't get a medal for this task.
forget the wrongs or failures you
see in a friend. To be able to say,
anything, and know you'll have the
same friend tomorrow. To share
your dreams with. To help them,
when they are feeling sorrow.

To encourge them when they are
unasure. warning them of constant
threats. Treating them like family
Is always the best.

If there close don't match, and they
got a funny smell. You let them know,
before somebody else can tell. The
people you meet, aren't really true
friends. True friends can't hurt you,
and be your friend till the end.

You never know how you look
through other peoples eyes. Being
open and honest to a friend, will give
you good vibes.

A true friend with Jesus, is the best
friend I'll ever know. I'll do my best
with my friends. Like Jesus does
to his own.

TESTIMONY

CHAPTER 12

The Job

If you want to live on this planet.
You got to have something to do.
You can't be a bum, and twiddle your thumbs.
You got to have some kind of job. Thats the rule.

You won't have any friends, if you don't listen.
Finding food and shelter is a must.
Just get a job, and do it well.
Then you'll have friends you can trust.

Doing a job for money is easy.
especailly if you don't have none.
Working with friends and helping them out.
Then your working just for fun.

Working with people, and making new friends.
Life is all about giving.
Then when your down and out. friends will help you out.
Thats why we are working on living.

TESTIMONY

CHAPTER 13

Earth

Nature works hard too. filling our souls with sun and shade. cleansing our blood from dirt and thirst. And with all the plants she waters with rain, and snow, Are so we can breath and eat. And when the land, gets too congested, she burns them up, so new life can grow. Hurricanes and floods and valcanos plays a big part of it too. We just so happens are in her way. Her water and land gives us food to eat. sunrise and sunset, land scapes galore. Gods art work never stops, and theres much more. A trillion creaures are sheltered and fed. Without human help. There are so many hidden things she does, that we don't understand. So, don't misuse her. Don't try and change her. Don't try and controll her. She might not like it, and She might do the opposite, of what she's does now. And, that would be beyond bad. God created this giant machine. He made it perfect. God even said, it was good.

TESTIMONY

CHAPTER 14

Old and New

In this modern world we live in,
and technology is in our hands.
We have computers, gps, and cell phones.
Faith in jesus, is not in our plans.

Now, life as we know it, is all mixed up.
Common since was easier back in Jesus day.
Saying the wrong thing, can get you killled.
Now, we have freedom of speech, All we'll get is tazed.

Robots can do our jobs, and our homes.
What are we going to do? Fly a kite?
Mankind will always find something to do.
We will rage war, and fight.

We won't have time to pray to God.
With out our cell phone, we will all be dum.
But, don't never forget, God has a plan.
Every one will be on there knees, when Jesus comes.

TESTIMONY

CHAPTER 15

The Wrong Way

This is a story about a man who wanted to conquer a mountain. As he stood at the bottom looking up. He said silently, lord, give me strength to do this. And got no answer. Then he thought, the first thing I got to do is get around those huge rocks thats in my way. Then I can start working my way up. As he walked torge the big rocks. They seem to be bigger than he first thought. He said, Lord, help me get around them. And still, got no answer. He started around the big rocks. Up and over, Up and over. The man slipped and sprung his ankle. As he cried out in pain. He saw a big tree limb that can support his weight. So he could continue his journey. He walked slower now, and was having a hard time. He stopped to rest, and looked down where he came from. He saw an empty field way below, ready for planting, and heard a still small voice in his head. Now is the time to plant our seeds. To help people understand the truth. To have a good harvest. To understand I am coming soon. That I am the ultimate farmer, that I will be with you. That I am the rock, and the crutch that holds you up. And I have a bigger mountain for you to conquer. The man raised his hand and praised the Lord, and headed back down saying to himself, I was going the wrong way. And had joy and peace in his heart. And planted many seeds.

The end

TESTIMONY

CHAPTER 1

Living In Space

Write first sentence of what this chapter is about here!

_____

_____

_____

_____

_____

_____

Write what you feel will be the last sentence of this chapter here!

_____

_____

_____

_____

_____

_____

CHAPTER 2

We Are Own Our Own

Write first sentence of what this chapter is about here!

_____

_____

_____

_____

_____

_____

Write what you feel will be the last sentence of this chapter here!

_____

_____

_____

_____

_____

_____

CHAPTER 3

Lessons Learned

Write first sentence of what this chapter is about here!

_____

_____

_____

_____

_____

_____

Write what you feel will be the last sentence of this chapter here!

_____

_____

_____

_____

_____

_____

_____

CHAPTER 4

Forever Young

Write first sentence of what this chapter is about here!

_____

_____

_____

_____

_____

_____

_____

Write what you feel will be the last sentence of this chapter here!

_____

_____

_____

_____

_____

_____

_____

_____

CHAPTER 5

World Of Peace

Write first sentence of what this chapter is about here!

_____

_____

_____

_____

_____

_____

Write what you feel will be the last sentence of this chapter here!

_____

_____

_____

_____

_____

_____

CHAPTER 6

World Of chaos

Write first sentence of what this chapter is about here!

_____

_____

_____

_____

_____

_____

Write what you feel will be the last sentence of this chapter here!

_____

_____

_____

_____

_____

_____

_____

CHAPTER 7

World We Live In

Write first sentence of what this chapter is about here!

_____

_____

_____

_____

_____

_____

Write what you feel will be the last sentence of this chapter here!

_____

_____

_____

_____

_____

_____

CHAPTER 8

How To Pray

Write first sentence of what this chapter is about here!

_____

_____

_____

_____

_____

_____

_____

Write what you feel will be the last sentence of this chapter here!

_____

_____

_____

_____

_____

_____

_____

CHAPTER 9

Work With People

Write first sentence of what this chapter is about here!

_____

_____

_____

_____

_____

_____

_____

Write what you feel will be the last sentence of this chapter here!

_____

_____

_____

_____

_____

_____

_____

_____

CHAPTER 10

Don't Miss The Boat

Write first sentence of what this chapter is about here!

_____

_____

_____

_____

_____

_____

Write what you feel will be the last sentence of this chapter here!

_____

_____

_____

_____

_____

_____

_____

CHAPTER 11

Friendship

Write first sentence of what this chapter is about here!

_____

_____

_____

_____

_____

_____

Write what you feel will be the last sentence of this chapter here!

_____

_____

_____

_____

_____

_____

_____

CHAPTER 12

The Job

Write first sentence of what this chapter is about here!

_____

_____

_____

_____

_____

_____

Write what you feel will be the last sentence of this chapter here!

_____

_____

_____

_____

_____

_____

CHAPTER 13

Earth

Write first sentence of what this chapter is about here!

_____

_____

_____

_____

_____

_____

Write what you feel will be the last sentence of this chapter here!

_____

_____

_____

_____

_____

_____

_____

CHAPTER 14

Old and New

Write first sentence of what this chapter is about here!

_____

_____

_____

_____

_____

_____

Write what you feel will be the last sentence of this chapter here!

_____

_____

_____

_____

_____

_____

CHAPTER 15

The Wrong Way

Write first sentence of what this chapter is about here!

_____

_____

_____

_____

_____

_____

Write what you feel will be the last sentence of this chapter here!

_____

_____

_____

_____

_____

_____